PILGRIM

PILGRIM

SECOND EDITION

Poems by DAVID WHYTE

20  19

MANY RIVERS PRESS

LANGLEY WASHINGTON

www.davidwhyte.com

Second Edition published 2014
by Many Rivers Press
P.O. Box 868
Langley WA 98260
USA

A catalogue record for this book
is available from the Library of Congress.

ISBN 978-1-932887-25-9

Printed in the United States of America

1st Printing 2012
2nd Edition 2014
3rd Printing 2016
4th Printing 2019
5th Printing 2020

For

CHARLOTTE MARY COTTER WHYTE

Beata et Pulcherrima Filia

Camino is dedicated to Lori De Mori. *The Aerialist* is dedicated
to Matilda Leyser and her new son. *The Well* is dedicated
to Marcia Cross. *Fifty* is dedicated to Patrick McCormack;
Finisterre to Marlene McCormack; *Etruscan Tomb* to
Leslie Cotter and Karin Backwell.
All the poems in the *COMPANION* chapter are dedicated to
the memory of John O' Donohue.

CONTENTS

CONTENTS *(continued)*

[1]

PILGRIM

PILGRIM

I bow to the lark
and its tiny
lifted silhouette
fluttering
before infinity.
I promise myself
to the mountain
and to the foundation
from which
my future comes.
I make my vow
to the stream
flowing beneath,
and to the water
falling
toward all thirst,
and
I pledge myself
to the sea
to which it goes
and to the mercy
of my disappearance,
and though I may be
left alone
or abandoned by
the unyielding present
or orphaned in some far
unspoken place,
I will speak
with a voice
of loyalty
and faith

to the far shore
where everything
turns to arrival,
if only in the sound
of falling waves
and I will listen
with sincere
and attentive eyes and ears
for a final invitation,
so that I can
be that note half-heard
in the flying lark song,
or that tint
on a far mountain
brushed with the subtle
grey of dawn,
even a river gone by
still looking
as if it hasn't,
or an ocean heard only
as the sound of waves
falling and falling,
and falling,
my eyes closing
with them
into some
undeserved nothing
even as they
give up their
strength
on the sand.

TRAVELLER

The heart's
a close-in horizon
that holds all distance
but gives
no explanation
to the tidal scour
of life
taking us
on and away
from the home
we know so well,
tearing us
from
the place
we tried to
inhabit
so firmly,
the anchorage
all gone,
the faces
all changed,
only the run and flow
of a life moving far
beyond
even the eternal voices
of those we love,
as if God
were all arrival
and
understood

only through
a weighted
tidal anticipation,
as if we were meant
to know
what we wanted
to know
only tomorrow,
as if we were,
after all,
from the very
beginning
born
far beyond
ourselves,
our whole being
a travelling
onward ghost,
that sees itself
only
in looking back,
always
just about
to find
a home,
always a
hairsbreadth
from
arrival,

always about
to find
the arms
that will never
fall away,
a self
as touch
and go,
a breath
and
an essence
hardly
ever held,
and
a visitation
able to
become real
only through
the miracle
fully
contained
in the
shift
from
this to *that*.

[II]

CAMINO

CAMINO

The way forward, the way between things,
the way already walked before you,
the path disappearing and re-appearing even
as the ground gave way beneath you,
the grief apparent only in the moment
of forgetting, then the river, the mountain,
the lifting song of the Sky Lark inviting
you over the rain filled pass when your legs
had given up, and after,
it would be dusk and the half-lit villages
in evening light; other people's homes
glimpsed through lighted windows
and inside, other people's lives; your own home
you had left crowding your memory
as you looked to see a child playing
or a mother moving from one side of
a room to another, your eyes wet
with the keen cold wind of Navarre.

But your loss brought you here to walk
under one name and one name only,
and to find the guise under which all loss can live;
remember, you were given that name every day
along the way, remember, you were greeted as such,
and treated as such and you needed no other name,
other people seemed to know you even before
you gave up being a shadow on the road
and came into the light, even before you sat down,
broke bread and drank wine,
wiped the wind-tears from your eyes:
pilgrim they called you,
pilgrim they called you again and again. Pilgrim.

REFUGE

Sometimes a nook, a wall half down,
a swerve in the path where the breeze
can't catch you; other times a made shelter,
a shepherd's build up of flat stones curved
to keep the wind off. Once, at the top of the pass,
it was a cave in the mountain rock taking you
in from the swirl and eddy of snow
and the killing cold so you could live
to a grey blank dawn.

Then in Galicia, it was a breath of warmth
from a kitchen door, palatial with light
and a daughter's smile; the family behind,
asking you in, as if to say, of all shelter,
traveller, you'll ever find on the road,
even with those you know,
the stranger's love is best of all.

REST

The bright of the moon before first light,
waking in the pre-dawn dark, the room illumined
and the edged, white, silver touch of sheets
sheer against the skin: the sense of having slept
wrapped in a blessing from the other side of night,
an unwarranted, gifted, messenger goodness;
a visitation as foundation and final destination,
the dark interior, invisible pulse, dissolving tiredness,
opening the eyes to a wakened world.

And after you were up, when the light had come
and the moon had gone, you found the path again
waiting through the open window, the faces at the table
gazing with you, as you sat with your coffee, silently
letting the sense of rest seat home, the body ready to walk,
in rhythm and in rhyme, with the given, unspoken source.

It was rest then, felt as sheer readiness, and the place
you went to find it, impossible to say, some artful way
the body looks for just repose after days of walking,
and only a few half images from the dream-hall
of sleep, a lantern swung, a voice speaking, inviting you in,
and then, a long welcome and heartfelt goodbye,
the crowd of faces sending you on, until you woke
to a morning pale with moonlight: snugged and warm
in your cell of hermetic completeness; your body
dedicated to anticipation, and to going on,
as if the way ahead had already been made for your feet,

as if there could have been
a hand on your back, all along, a parallel
that was not a parallel, some internal invisible way
you had to walk; and always with you, a listening in:
an echo in the dark to take along the lighted road.

NIGHT TRAVELLER

Until this loss,
the clear moon
had always been there,
now a growing sphere
illuminating your way,
now a flit of light
showing nothing
but the shadowed outline
of the trees
and the cloudy opalescence
of the distant sky,
but now came
the three days
and three nights
with no moon at all,
hidden as it was
behind the very earth
you walked, your feet
looking for purchase
as you stumbled
on the roots of trees,
so that you felt as if bereft
and betrayed
even by the darkness
that had been your friend,
cut off by the night
whose mercies had held you
in the close circle of its arms
and hidden you from sight
of the sleeping world
you passed,

no by then
it seemed
even the night
had made itself
an enemy
to your onward way
as if it wanted
to stop you travelling
to meet them,
as if it wanted,
against your will
to keep them from you,
as if it was asking you
to stay and make a shelter,
so that your rebellion
in the end
was against the day
and the night,
and the sun
and the moon
and every season
of the turning sky
no matter
what it seemed
to want of you,
until you heard
your own voice
in the shadows saying
you didn't want to stop,

didn't want
to be seen
in the light of day,
didn't want
to light a fire
and warm yourself,
didn't believe you deserved
to warm yourself,
wanted only the comfortable
onward way in the dark,
the stillness and the closeness
to those you'd lost,
and the final dark hall
you wanted to traverse
where you knew they lived;
to knock at last on the door
to your own disappearance
and arrive at their side at last.

THE WELL

Be thankful now for having arrived,
for the sense of having drunk from a well,
for remembering the long drought
that preceded your arrival and the years
walking in a desert landscape of surfaces
looking for a spring hidden from you so long
that even wanting to find it now had gone
from your mind until you only remembered
the hard pilgrimage that brought you here,
the thirst that caught in your throat;
the taste of a world just-missed
and the dry throat that came from a love
you remembered but had never fully wanted
for yourself, until finally after years making
the long trek to get here it was as if your whole
achievement had become nothing but thirst itself.

But the miracle had come simply
from allowing yourself to know
that you had found it, that this time
someone walking out into the clear air
from far inside you had decided not to walk
past it any more; the miracle had come
at the roadside in the kneeling to drink
and the prayer you said, and the tears you shed
and the memory you held and the realization
that in this silence you no longer had to keep
your eyes and ears averted from the place
that could save you, that you had been given
the strength to let go of the thirsty dust laden
pilgrim-self that brought you here, walking

with her bent back, her bowed head
and her careful explanations.

No, the miracle had already happened
when you stood up, shook off the dust
and walked along the road from the well,
out of the desert toward the mountain,
as if already home again, as if you deserved
what you loved all along, as if just
remembering the taste of that clear cool
spring could lift up your face and set you free.

NOT TAKEN

The path you did not take,
ran with you for a while,
just the other side of the mountain,
or meandering with you on the far bank
of the onward river you followed;
the sound of its flowing water holding
your respective journeys together,
as if its merciful but distant companionship
could always move with you;
always be with you,
waiting for you to cross over
as you always meant to,
when this path you had followed
had come to an end.

But you never turned to cross,
and you never found a bridge,
and you never took that other way,
and you stayed on this path to the end,
recalling the other way you did not take
as you would a close and loving friend
who had left you not to leave you but simply
to go on with their life, so that you carried
their memory through the years that passed
as you would a beautiful and worthwhile burden,
growing with them as they grew,
walking with them as they walked,
until one day it was just as if that someone
you had come to love at a distance,

and that someone who had walked with you
always on the other side of the stream,
had passed away, but in your mind you were
still speaking to them and still walking with them
and still carrying them onward, but now
just a short way to a place you would lay them down,
under the trees, and in a way in which memory
and everyday presence stop living in separate worlds,
and the calm, death-still image of every disappearance,
renews itself in some extraordinary beginning again,
and you realize, sitting by their side, saying goodbye,
that you took no separate path at all,
neither this nor that, neither the one you loved
nor the one you did not want, that you had after all,
always held them generously together
by not choosing this side of existence or the other.

You were in the end,
never just looking on,
but always the river moving between
and the song of the water,
holding the flowing of ways together.

SANTIAGO

The road seen, then not seen, the hillside
hiding then revealing the way you should take,
the road dropping away from you as if leaving you
to walk on thin air, then catching you, holding you up,
when you thought you would fall,
and the way forward always in the end
the way that you followed, the way that carried you
into your future, that brought you to this place,
no matter that it sometimes took your promise from you,
no matter that it had to break your heart along the way:
the sense of having walked from far inside yourself
out into the revelation, to have risked yourself
for something that seemed to stand both inside you
and far beyond you, that called you back
to the only road in the end you could follow, walking
as you did, in your rags of love and speaking in the voice
that by night became a prayer for safe arrival,
so that one day you realized that what you wanted
had already happened long ago and in the dwelling place
you had lived in before you began,
and that every step along the way, you had carried
the heart and the mind and the promise
that first set you off and drew you on and that you were
more marvelous in your simple wish to find a way
than the gilded roofs of any destination you could reach:
as if, all along, you had thought the end point might be a city
with golden towers, and cheering crowds,
and turning the corner at what you thought was the end
of the road, you found just a simple reflection,

and a clear revelation beneath the face looking back
and beneath it another invitation, all in one glimpse:
like a person and a place you had sought forever,
like a broad field of freedom that beckoned you beyond;
like another life, and the road still stretching on.

FINISTERRE

The road in the end taking the path the sun had taken,
into the western sea, and the moon rising behind you
as you stood where ground turned to ocean: no way
to your future now but the way your shadow could take,
walking before you across water, going where shadows go,
no way to make sense of a world that wouldn't let you pass
except to call an end to the way you had come,
to take out each frayed letter you had brought
and light their illumined corners; and to read
them as they drifted on the late western light;
to empty your bags; to sort this and to leave that;
to promise what you needed to promise all along,
and to abandon the shoes that brought you here
right at the water's edge, not because you had given up
but because now, you would find a different way to tread,
and because, through it all, part of you would still walk on,
no matter how, over the waves.

[III]

COMPANION

THE WAVE

You arrived as a ripple of change emanating
from an original, unstoppable,
memory, a then made now,
entirely yourself, found now in the world,
now as creator of that world,
you were a signature written in sand
taken by the ocean and scattered
to another wave form, your disappearance
only made more beautiful
by the everyday arrival of a tide
where my voice can still join yours,
hungering for the fall of water,
so that walking the reflected sand,
I set myself to learn by your going,
knowing across death's wide ocean,
the ultimate parallel to friendship.

BREATH

Once we had returned,
as if from the dead ourselves,
talking in low voices
at the table
where you lay looking
upward,
your handsome face
severe with the beauty
of stillness
and the half smile
we knew so well.

Once we had seen
your profile lifted
toward us
in the old way
you had
when just
about to speak.

Once we had sat
by you again,
a crowd of living faces
round the calm
unmoving angel
you had strangely become,

we who could hardly
believe you gone,
looked at one another
above the breathless,
unmoving body,
as if astonished by
the absence
of breath itself.

The give and the take,
the easy in and out
the casual exchange
of elements,
the *this* for *that*,
our easy speech
surrounding you,
sending you on.

But inwardly I said,
What has made me
will be given back,
what I have loved
was loved because it was not me,
but changed me,
even as it left me,
and you who leave me now
show mercy in your going
by stirring the memory
of your first arrival.

Even in the first inward cry
I made, hearing
I had lost you,
I gave myself
to that living air,
to friendship,
and to what
I could never hold.

REQUIEM

Driving away
from your quiet body
through the pre-dawn dark
and the low roar
of the heater, still blowing chill
in the cold interior
of the dial-lit car,
the field walls illuminated
as if by passing eyes alone,
I followed the mountain road
over the bends
and the pitch black crest
of the winterage,
seeing the lit, cold stone,
on either side
of the empty road,
where I could drive
in the freedom of
the early hours,
left or right
of the middle line
anywhere
I wanted,
and still stunned
and immobile
at the thought of you
there
and the quiet rested
nobility of your form
left alone to sleep
forever,

I suddenly felt
the pure note
of you in me,
a pitch that had me held
and quiet,
as if the choir
that had sung
unheard in me
these last days
had touched at last
the held note
that leaves a chapel silent,
so that the stones
and the rock
and the white wells
and the clear austerity
of prayer surrounding me
seemed like an ally
and a friend at last,
no landscape to overcome
but my home and rest
so that though I drove away
from you through a land
you knew
and that you
wouldn't want to leave,
I felt as if
you were looking with me,
though I left you
you were coming with me,

as if my life lay not one side
of your going
or the other,
but here
in the pained
and pilgrim present,
as if we still
had an arm,
each around
the other,
you in the light
and me in the dark
taking turn
and turn again
to help each other see,
our breath pluming
together
in the cold air
of the car
as we sat together
as we had before,
prayerful,
parallel
inhabitants
of an onward way,
now hallowed
by the power
of distance.

GLENTRASNA

When the music started, I wondered
where it came from, the low haunt
of an air carried on the careless wind,
the lift of a jackdaw caught by a breeze
from the mountain, someone
was playing the flute hidden by a wall,
not knowing that anyone, anywhere,
could listen in, walking through
the simplest song that seemed to need
the broadest, clearest, upland sky.

I listened then, to the rarest of music,
the one played for no one.
Every hesitation and every step
the haunting took across the sky was let alone
to touch its full eternal measure;
every note allowed to float beyond itself
to a world with no approaching end.

There was no looking for the right
beginning, no search for the perfect close,
and no listener but the player
themselves beyond all listening,
so that I felt in that modal harmony
of stone and grass and mountain sky
and the clear view across the blue lake
below as if I stood alone and entire
with a world held in place, as if
memory could be true, and horizons
hold their own unspoken promise,
and that grief might be its own cure.

And in the last held moment before
the music stopped and left the mountain
to itself, and the final, un-final note slurred
into the raptured air, as if the deepest pain
could be a long way to somewhere after all,
and of all things, this already knowing,
never quite fully broken
barely open but breathing heart,
the one to serve me best.

TRESPASSES

Your presence is the invitational mystery
it always was, a half-disappearance
even when you lived and breathed
and walked beside us in the lighted day.

You were here and gone as much then
as you are now except the door
will never open now to see you enter
and call out loud in the way you could,

though your voice still carries
an insistent whisper, close to my ear.
I dreamt the other night I was in some
divine and ordinary classroom

explaining your whole life to you,
the one you had lived, everything
you had done, all you had written,
everyone you had touched,

when you turned to me
and took me by the shoulder
and looked into my eyes
and laughed in realization, saying,

and you were a good friend to me weren't you?
And I woke up with tears in my eyes, as if
to dream more would presume upon the new life
that had asked you, so suddenly to leave this one.

Did I know you even before I met you?
Are first meetings some frontier
already existing in the world
to which both are invited

and without which
neither could have existed?
Friendship abides through
mutual and repeated forgiveness

and we were brought to forgive again
and again, letters, phone calls, the difficulties
of closeness and distance—the wrong word
about the right word—but forgive we always did

as we had to, our trespasses against each other
transfigured in the end by the endless meal,
the filled glass, an accolade, a laugh or an exclamation,
the hands extended, high above the table,

and like our eyes, firmly locked together,
as if to say, *There is something we do not know*
about the way we were sent as companion voices
to walk this world, together or apart.

But your death strained the sinews of
that bond again and left me helpless
to know how fully to forgive your going
when I had not yet fully forgiven you.

I write this then to set the table for us both,
to lay out glasses, full plates, to pour the wine, to
     laugh
and cry out loud as we did. Shake hands now,
I'll give you your death if you give me mine.

BLESSING (FOR ONE WHO BLESSED)

May your palms be as good for blessing
now as when you lived and breathed,
may your voice still carry us as you used
to carry us when you filled a room
with laughter and we rode the tide
of your arriving shout.

May there be a way to bless from the place
you inhabit, may you extend your hands
and your old way of speaking from the horizon
where you live, and may you remember us
and bless us here, in this place, and in this time
in the lit room of our present imaginations
or in the reflected glass, lifted to you
or to one another, remembering you;
and wondering if you still remember us.

And as you have travelled the way before us,
may you bless us especially on the long road
that starts from these words, in our meetings
and in our partings, in our simple wish to find a way
and especially, in our visible and invisible arrivals.

And because we have still to cross the threshold
that you have passed and make the journey
that you have completed, and because
we do not know from where you bless or even
if you still can bless, we need those words of yours
and that voice of yours, and the merciful world
behind that voice, and your laughter and your hands
turned toward us, as strong and as good as they ever were.

[IV]

THE WEST

STAR

North of Oughterard
there comes a sudden
lapse and steal of light
in the sky, the opening
of an invitation
to a different way
through land
once thought familiar,
and driving on
into the low western sun
the sense of
a parallel looked for
but not yet found,
the crack between the world
as you want it
and the world you
seem to have inherited,
the evening light beginning
to pale everything,
and the great discipline
remembering
to drive the road
into that disappearing
gleam and not lose sight
of the beckoning
interior horizon,
never to pass the door
to the liminal world,
but to go another
different way,

through Conamara
far from the traffic
that slows the mind
and the grey lash
of habit that feeds
our disappointment;
to drive and never
let the eyes fall once
to check the blurring screen,
but remember
to practice
the nobility
that comes with promise,
to drive out west,
the eyes level or lifted
the mind cleared;
the steering wheel
invisible
below the eye
but still
charting the needed course
and the body at tiptoe,
leaning toward
the windscreen,
the breath held
and the eyes
a-shiver for
a falling plume of sky;

the clear, pinpoint star
that just appeared
above Leenane,
one you
did not realize
you were following.

THOOR ANU

You did not know you had come
to meet the ocean,

thinking the cliff edge
had everything you'd need,

but when you stared into
the deep vault

of blue from which the revelation
came

and you heard the drumbeat
of arriving water

and looked into
the bowl

of waves and breaking foam,
and sat there stunned

and numb in the underbelly
of the turning world

the vision
was immediate,

a ghost-like far-in horizon
come to meet the sea

an anchored, internal origination
equal to the sway of moon

or ocean or even the wind itself
blowing in from nowhere

an interior
living the edge as center

and the pulse of two great hearts,
beating together,

with the waves' arrival
and the bird flight

and the choir inside me
singing with the ocean,

the rising inward tide
a lifting and a washing away

and a first footing,
in some *terra incognita*,

a castaway sense of self,
once wrested and blown away,

now strangely re-ordered and restored
like a fulcrum

from which all movement
could come,

like a door you did not realize
was already open,

like a robust and gifted
helplessness,

a low, mounting ocean roar
growing from within,

an elemental undoing
you'd carry with you

in the city street
or the plane ride home,

still newly inhabited
in the small hours

of the quiet night or the hubbub
of a crowded room,

as if everything felt there
is happening still

as an anticipation
a slow,

rolling arrival of waves,
a birthing,

a life delineated. Before and after
Thoor Anu.

LON'S FORT

is round and looks
on every other roundness
of the world
as if to stand here
is to stand
at the center
of circle
after growing circle
and reach
in the mind
for a far circumference
that holds as focus
an interior so far in
so concentrated
with origin
we find ourselves
by looking out
at what looks back:
the lighted edge
of rock and sky,
the sweet
unmoving darkness
over the horizon
that makes
a perfect
beckoning symmetry
to the night
beneath our feet,
the underground

where light cannot live
but whose darkness
makes a ground
on which to stand,
the central
ancestral story
of those who
lived here
looking out
at the same
horizon
and the same
surrounding
ground
who saw a world
that witnessed them
at a privileged
center,
their lives caught
like ours
in the glance
of what lies beyond
only
for
a fleeting
moment.

FIFTY

New mown,
the great pale gold
stretch of field
revealed beneath
the absent barley
like a lovely upturned face
already starred with green
from the clover
growing to replace it—
and with the harvest done,
the mower parked
and the field
left to silence,
the dogs bound happily
in the cleared space
while Patrick stands,
head thrown back
in laughter by the gate.

Sometimes we are surprised
by the steal and turn
of beauty
through a working life,
the ruffling wind
stirring the barley
behind backs
bent in worldly concentration,
thinking we had planted
just to eat and sell,

forgetting the way things
meet and conspire
round the focused endeavor.

That daughter
standing with us
we thought we knew,
grown into womanhood
while the field is sown,
or a partner's face,
harvest within harvest,
softened by age
our eyes renewed
by a sudden
and unfamiliar, familiar.

And then this new mown field
close to the house
stretched away now
to some
horizon
beyond all attempt
to bring one year
to a recognized harvest.

And no end time now
looking at the cleared field,
no time at all
but time as if collapsed

and concentrated
around us,
stunning us to quiet
through the hush and light
of absence itself,
the gold wave of barley
come and gone,
the cutting away of the ripe
and ready to go
revealing beneath
like a breath not taken,
like a thought not fully made,
like the year ahead
not yet lived,
the minted
clover,
green and new,
and ourselves
together
looking on
as if living in a gifted,
unlooked for
second life,
seeing again
how
an empty cup
can brim once more
to the gleam,

like some miracle at Cana
and we the guests
having witnessed
everything taken away,
expectant only of winter,
ready to turn away,
saw
spring laid bare
right
beneath it;
then stood together
hands on each other's shoulders
the chrism of the sight
in our eyes,
all expectation felled
and grown,
ready in a moment
to believe again.

BROTHERS

(Overheard in MacNeil's, Ballyvaughan)

Listen to me now, I have the right to ask,
on the day the sun goes down on the grey city
and you feel the weight bear down again.

And look at me now, while the drink is on you
and has you honest for a moment,
don't take the lonely road you walked before,

the one that took you and wouldn't give you back
but ask me, when it all comes over you, to lift you up
and make you laugh with some old confidence.

And listen, most of all, even in the soothing glow
of a laptop screen, or the guttering sound of a mobile
     phone;
by a shouted hail from the bar, covering the manful hurt,

or crawling to my front door on your hands and knees
like a desperate, weeping Thersites, *make me drive you*
to the mountain above Aughinish when the light is falling

sideways from the western sea and the clouds are
mounding above themselves, and our faces can be lit
again with memory, you and I together

driving along the way, falling into the silence
we've worked so hard to learn to live through,
knowing, when we've parked at Rossalie,

we'll walk the high green road above the bay
and catch the ebbing light that does you good
and strengthen your memory and lead your eye

to the ocean and the gleaming stretching strand and stop
and sit and watch the tiny cars below, going nowhere,
while we in parallel go somewhere above, moving quietly

on the quiet road in the swim and glance and sweep
of the evening rays; your eyes looking through it all
to that grey misted nowhere across the bay—

Conamara—you always say, as if heaven
had come into your life again *and so it will,*
like a great cure, a new start. *No, no, listen,*

you know just a glance of rain in your face,
just a walk down the mountain for a first pint
near midnight in the late murmur of MacNeil's

can set you straight, even just a brief moment
of laughter out of nowhere can be enough
to turn you round. *Look at you now—good as gold.*

So come and see me, calling out whatever you want,
calling me whatever you want, *eejit, brother, friend,* you know
I have known you forever and you have known nothing

since you were born without knowing me.
I have loved you like another self since you were
the youngest thing when I used to put my arm round you

to nurse you home, the knees broken and the world
fallen in, the pushed bicycle a moving, clacking ruin,
and you leaning against me, as you still must now.

No, listen, listen to me now, You know you must go
nowhere without me for a good while
until the wound is staunched and held

by familiarity and friendship, us two
the only ones left who know
the necessary history, *we, the only ones*

able to find the cure, by leaning against each
other, by the brushed shoulders
finding each other by accident or design,

and the laughter breaking again through held grief,
but above all you must know I am *here* now,
only to keep you *here,* you must know, when we get
      there

looking down from Patrick's Well,
love still lives and sings like the lark song above our
      heads,
and love still calls you to stay with me.

You must know, even in the West,
even in the breathless moon of a North Clare night,
I am nowhere unless I am beside you.

FUGITIVE

From the shelter
of the stone
walled corner
where calves
moon at dusk
for the short
spring grass,
look out from
your high stone place
at Ireton's
troop searching
the mauve bog light;
watch them
indifferent to
the ardour
of a new season
breaking
through limestone
and fern cleft,
traversing the
grike and grain
of a white Burren
made black
and shining
by late rain,
and the soft
metamorphosis
of water
falling past them

through
what looks like surface
into the hidden
landscape beneath,
the underground
that keeps you safe,
the souterrain
of drip and drown,
where one can listen
to the horsemen
searching above,
while you call
on Mary and Joseph
and Conor O'Brien
and the honour
of your father
and look down at them,
through the cold run,
of that single
necessary tear,
the slow
travelling revelation
of damp decline
touching cheek and chin
that falls
under the gravity of loss
into some heady, stone
cathedral dark-space
holding everything above.

Why show yourself
to the world
when everything real
has foundations
not seen by light?

When under-neathness
holds everything
in some deep
sacred non-space?

Why try to be
any new origin
when spring seems
to do it all regardless
of the death
of loved ones
or the cry
for mercy?

Why go on,
when newness
still comes
from nowhere,
growing even
through grief

and the indifferent
warming light,
barely willed,
still brings spring
purpled with gentian
and trefoil
and the green cress
bubbling
in water
by the
blesséd well?

Why stir at all
when season
and age
and heartbreak
does it all?

Tempting to assume
the shape made
in staying hidden,
the crookback stance,
the pursed lips
and the limbs
gripping stone
like unforgiving ivy,
tempting to make
a life in shadow now,
a gripping
growing round
that hangs on

only to what
can be remembered,
to give up,
to go where others
went before
into some
other parallel,
that other
invisible light
that catches
only the harshness
of your face,
as you sup
in satisfaction
in the quiet hall
where the
Tuatha
sat before you,
waiting to come
into the world again,
a tempting
internal exile
kept at bay
while you catch
the beckoning
sense
of a rising tide,

and the need to
rise and go,
a gusted, caught
wherewithal suddenly
within you
to join the others,
another wild goose
lifting its head
above the stone lake
sensing a distant shore,
wanting to leave and return
renewed by the wind,
here and gone,
away and beyond
over the sea.

Go now,
before you
understand
this island
and this world
and its future
only through
the small triumph
granted
by squinting
through stone.

[v]

LOOKING BACK

SECOND LIFE

My uncourageous life
doesn't want to go,
doesn't want to speak,
doesn't want to carry on,
wants to make its way
through stealth,
wants to assume
the strange and dubious honor
of not being heard.

My uncourageous life
doesn't want to move,
doesn't even want to stir,
wants to inhabit
a difficult form
of stillness,
to pull everything
into the silence
where the throat strains
but gives no voice.

My uncourageous life
wants to stop
the whole world
and keep it stopped
not only for itself
but for everyone
and everything it knows,
refusing to stir a single inch
until given an exact
and final destination.

This uncourageous
second life wants to win
some undeserved lottery
so that it can finally
bestow a just and final
reward upon itself.

No, this second life
never wants to write
or speak, or cook
or set the table
or welcome guests
or sit up talking
with a stranger
who might accidently
set us travelling again.

This second life
doesn't want
to leave the door,
doesn't want
to take any path
that works its own
sweet way
through mountains,
doesn't want
to follow
the beckoning flow
of a distant river
nor meet
the chance weather

where a pass
takes us
from one discovered
world
to another.

This second life
just wants to lie down;
close its eyes
and tell God
it has a headache.

But my other life
my first life,
the life I admire
and want to follow
looks on and listens
with some wonder,
and even extends
a reassuring hand
for the one holding back,
knowing there can be
no real confrontation
without the need
to turn away
and go back
away from it all,
to have things
be different,

and to close our eyes
until they
are different.

No,
this hidden life,
this first courageous life,
seems to speak
from silence
and in the language
of a knowing,
beautiful heartbreak,
above all
it seems to know
well enough
it will have
to give back
everything received
in any form
and even, sometimes,
as it tells the story
of the way ahead,
laughs out loud
in the knowledge.

This first life seems
sure and steadfast
in knowing
it will come across
the help it needs

at every crucial place
and thus continually
sharpens my sense
of impending
revelation.

This first
courageous life
in fact, has already
gone ahead
has nowhere to go
except
out the door
into the clear air
of morning
taking me with it,
nothing to do
except to breathe
while it can,
no way to travel
but with that familiar
pilgrim
movement in the body,
nothing to teach except
to show me
on the long road
how we sometimes
like to walk alone,
open to the silent revelation,

and then stop and gather
and share everything
as dark comes in,
telling the story
of a day's accidental
beauty.

And perhaps
most intriguingly
and most poignantly
and most fearfully of all
and at the very end
of the long road
it has travelled,
it wants to take me
to a high place
from which to see,
with a view looking back
on the way we took
to get there,
so it can have me
understand myself
as witness
and thus
bequeath me
the way ahead,
so it can teach me
how to invent
my own disappearance

so it can lie down at the end
and show me,
even against my will,
how to undo myself,
how to surpass myself:
how to find
a way
to die
of generosity.

BORN AGAIN

I want to be born again but I want to be born
exactly the selfsame way, with both feet
on ground I know, seeing a purple line of moor
edging my father's Yorkshire; or standing there,
dumbstruck and dumbfounded on the edge
of my mother's turf, looking out
from Thoor Anu, over the boiling surf to Aran.

I want to be born again, but I want to be born exactly
as I was, almost between things, as I was in this life,
and as I want to be in the next: Mary Teresa O'Sullivan,
nine months gone, carrying me back to England,
her pains sharp in Waterford, sharper in Dublin,
the hard rolling bench of the ferry almost my midwife.

I want to be born again so that I can hear
the familiar sounds again, but this time
know what I am hearing from the inside out,
that first beckoning roar of the sea,
then the firmness of footsteps on land,
and after, in that hidden, hill-bound house,
my mother's singing voice, then my sisters' first words
and my father's voice at the lighted door.

I want to be born again so that I can see
every face again, my new father, desperate, looking
to find me through a ward room window,
my grandmother's eyes searching out time
on a far church clock, haloed by light,
the surprise of my grandfather's grief
passed to me and to me alone.

I want to be young and start it all again
but this time I want to deserve my youth,
to study generosity, to watch my mind
grow supple, to conjugate the verbs
that mark the body's joyful round
and anticipate even my heartbreak
by thinking of the loves ahead.

I want to work again and I want to earn
again and I want to write again
but above all I'll want all the uncalled for
invisible help again: a strong wind always
to take me home, a mother's fierce intent,
her swollen gift, held until land,
and the food put before me on a hundred,
hundred, tables, all the hands and the strangers
and the teachers that taught me,
or even struck me, or held me safe.

I want to be born again, in exactly the selfsame life,
aware this time from the inside out, and to stand this time
as a beautiful un-worrying witness, living beyond
the need for this or that; some memory always with me
of a ship making its way through lifting water,
the song of the wind, the song of my mother,
my father's disbelieving, expectant face,
and the crowding, merciful voice of the sea at my birth.

UNLEAVENED

Looking
back
at you
standing
there,
wind swept
on an edge
of grey
northern
moor
you were
just
one step away
from what
you wanted,
Tir na nog
through
a bank
of mist,
the voice
calling you
there
all right
but
indistinct,
the half
perceived
angel
flitting

in the grey
wind curl
of a northern
sky
always
present
always
opening
her hand
to you,
and
you were
already
half way there
in one sense
already
fully realized
in another
waiting for
everything
to happen,
and for you
everything
was
an omen,
a presage,
a first possible
invitation,
now,

my first
thought
looking back
at you
is to be
that revelatory
angel
my self
and
out
of the
rain laden sky
put
my hand
in yours,
to help you over
the threshold
into this
future
I now inhabit
and which
strangely
I inherited
from you,
but
the first
touch
of your hand
always transfigures

as if you were
waiting
for me
all along
to come back
and find you,
and I realize
standing
here
in the rain
and wind,
the two
of us
come together
through all
difficulties
in one
sheltering
body
at last
that
only through
your eyes
would
I ever
want
to live
the future
again.

ETRUSCAN TOMB

There are places that seem
to expect us:
to take us in like pilgrims
from the way ahead
to tell us suddenly
and without fanfare
of a new beginning
made out of nothing
but the way we got here,
as if the hard road
of difficulty and despair
and minor triumph
that brought us here
could make sense
simply by the nature
of a particular geographic
welcome,
like this spur of olive grove
overlooking the Val di Paese,
its upright stones cradled
on the ridge
by a surrounding hollow,
so that the tomb
feels like two hands
cupped together
holding
the flow of remembrance,
so that we drink,
the never ending spring

hardly knowing what we drink
and look out at the quiet groves
not knowing
what we see,
taking the cup
from our ancestors
as they took it
from their ancestors
and their ancestors
before them,
each generation first grieving
and then respecting, forgetting
and then remembering again
how the chain of life is forged,
how what we love
and leave behind
becomes more real to others
because we hold it
knowing
how it flows away
and in a place like this
each of us can recall
the clear memory of a young son
or growing daughter
or a good friend
let go into the world,
recall
a parent who
watched over us,
year after year

who blessed us
simply by
asking after us,
who watched us
in our youthful
affections,
as our hands folded
in newness
next to our hearts,
caught in
the surprising
tide that trapped us
and freed us
from ourselves,
the secret harvest
growing inside:
the ripening,
uncaring
blossoms of desire
that disturbed
our quiet hours;
and the night
visitations of lovers
never to return.

And then,
and only in looking back,
the sudden miraculous
sense of the circle
that made us whole,

the sisters or the brothers
or the distant cousins
we played with as children,
the father or the mother
or the mothers
before mothers, ancestral,
handed down, ours.

Even here,
in the solemn stately
commitment
of wife and husband
we find
the ancient
declaration
to the unspeakable
promise,
the unknown
darkness
to which we eventually,
make our way.

We stopped
to say a simple word
of thanks that we could walk
to this place and find it
like a promised
understanding,
like an intuition long held,
that it stood always

at the end
of the long road
we took to get here
as if to welcome us;
as if to teach and hold us
in this time, now,
to understand at last,
how close the threshold
is that takes us
like a blessing
from a world
we think we know
and turns our face
to wonder
by the gift
of a sheer
imagined absence,
the twilight sense
of the ultimate purification,
to love and let go.

Arriving at the tomb
we imagined their lives
and now we try to
re-imagine ours.

Becoming,
as we stand
together
in some sincere
remembrance,
the promised future
that finally
inherits their gifts.

WINTER APPLE

Let the apple ripen
on the branch
beyond your need
to take it down.

Let the coolness
of autumn
and the breathing,
blowing wind
test its adherence
to endurance,
let the others fall.

Wait longer
than you would,
go against yourself,
find the pale nobility
of quiet that ripening
demands,
watch with patience
as the silhouette emerges
and the leaves fall,
see it become
a solitary roundness
against a greying sky,
let winter come
and the first
frost threaten,
and then wake
one morning

to see the breath
of winter
has haloed
its redness
with light.

So that a full
two months
after you
should have
taken the apple
down,
you hold it in
your closed hand
at last and bite
into the cool
sweetness
spread evenly
through every
single atom
of a pale
and yielding
structure,
so that you taste
on that cold,
grey day,
not only
the after reward
of a patience
remembered,

not only
the summer
sunlight
of a postponed
perfection,
but the sweet,
inward stillness
of the wait itself.

SECOND SIGHT

Sometimes, you need the ocean light,
    and colors you've never seen before
        painted through an evening sky.

Sometimes you need your God
    to be a simple invitation,
        not a telling word of wisdom.

Sometimes you need only the first shyness
    that comes from being shown things
        far beyond your understanding,

so that you can fly and become free
    by being still and by being still here.

And then there are times you need to be
    brought to ground by touch
        and touch alone.

To know those arms around you
    and to make your home in the world
        just by being wanted.

To see those eyes looking back at you,
    as eyes should see you at last,

seeing you, as you always wanted to be seen,
    seeing you, as you yourself
        had always wanted to see the world.

THE AERIALIST

She was a bird in flight,
a pair of young wings,
a nest just left, and a horizon
almost imagined,
in her freedom she gave us
an arc that can only exist
as the far edge
of some invisible center
that holds all travel.

Though we sat below
as she flew on,
she was proof
of some anchorage
that could hold us
through all aloneness,
the way we long,
in front of watching eyes
to take an extraordinary,
airy, courageous step
holding the coercive
laws of ground at bay.

Imagine our surprise
then, looking on,
the way it came to fullness,

not in some
breath defying
disappearance
in the tented sky,
nor in some twist and run
that bent our following necks,
but when she slipped to earth,
so quietly, without fanfare,
her satin foot
gliding to ground
like a whisper,
as if to say,
you too can land like this,
as I did, just now,
remade in your arrival
but quiet, unassuming,
able to take the familiar hurt,
once again
of being here and being found,
can come to earth
as if grounding lightly
on the sand of a new world,
re-imagined and witnessed
and reborn
as you were,
by that flight
you made against the sky.

[VI]

POSTSCRIPT

FINTAN

The pool near Slane where hazel brushes the gleam of water
and the just ripe nut touches and un-touches the still
cold darkness of a shaded stream, the wet
encircled shell a meniscus of light for the rising mouth
of a silvered salmon, scale and sleek. The moon,
the wait, the strike, the plash of dawn-lit water,
whoever ate this fish that fed on the tree of life,
whoever caught and cooked and then consumed
the flesh of the messenger god, would make no king,
would uncover no gold to hoard against the coming awe,
would become mortal-wise through words enfleshed
with the nut of truth, would become equal to the task
of living and dying, a man acknowledged,
as one who *could* now speak for others, who *would* now
speak for others, greatest of poets in a land of poets.

Discover more about David Whyte's work, including walking tours, public speaking engagements and working with organizations.

MANY RIVERS
PO Box 868
Langley WA 98260
USA

360.221.1324
www.davidwhyte.com
mrivers@davidwhyte.com